CW00495834

WHY HASN'T GOD HEALED ME?

How faith and persistence can bring healing and wholeness to all of us

Glenys Godfrey

WHY HASN'T GOD HEALED ME?

How faith and persistence can bring healing and wholeness to all of us

Glenys Godfrey

MEREO
Cirencester

Mereo Books
1A The Wool Market Dyer Street Cirencester Gloucestershire GL7 2PR
An imprint of Memoirs Publishing www.mereobooks.com

Why hasn't God healed me?: 978-1-86151-513-1

First published in Great Britain in 2016
by Mereo Books, an imprint of Memoirs Publishing

Copyright ©2016

Glenys Godfrey has asserted her right under the Copyright Designs and Patents Act 1988 to be identified as the author of this work.

This book is a work of fiction and except in the case of historical fact any resemblance to actual persons living or dead is purely coincidental.

A CIP catalogue record for this book is available from the British Library.

This book is sold subject to the condition that it shall not by way of trade or otherwise be lent, resold, hired out or otherwise circulated without the publisher's prior consent in any form of binding or cover, other than that in which it is published and without a similar condition, including this condition being imposed on the subsequent purchaser.

The address for Memoirs Publishing Group Limited can be found at www.memoirspublishing.com

The Memoirs Publishing Group Ltd Reg. No. 7834348

The Memoirs Publishing Group supports both The Forest Stewardship Council® (FSC®) and the PEFC® leading international forest-certification organisations. Our books carrying both the FSC label and the PEFC® and are printed on FSC®-certified paper. FSC® is the only forest-certification scheme supported by the leading environmental organisations including Greenpeace. Our paper procurement policy can be found at www.memoirspublishing.com/environment

Typeset in 12/20pt Century Schoolbook
by Wiltshire Associates Publisher Services Ltd. Printed and bound in Great Britain
by Printondemand-Worldwide, Peterborough PE2 6XD

MIX
Paper from responsible sources
FSC® C004959
PEFC

This little book was written to encourage and assist those seeking healing. Remember, God loves you and wants you well. Don't give up.

Dedicated to my good friend Jean Attwood, without whose help it would not have been written.

Please note that all scripture is taken from the New King James Version and Strong's Concordance of the Bible

CONTENTS

THE THINGS PEOPLE SAY

'God is sovereign, so He can't want me healed.'

'My mother died of heart disease, so I probably will. It runs in the family.'

'The doctors say I have 6 months to live but I'm believing for my healing.'

'I have been prayed for many times and nothing has worked.'

'I have been a churchgoer all my life and God still hasn't healed me.'

'The whole congregation prayed and prayed and the vicar's wife still died.'

'I'm a good person and kind to animals. Why has God made me sick?'

'God has made me sick to teach me something. I can see it has made me a better person.'

'God made me sick so I would be more sympathetic to sick people.'

'God made Job sick, didn't He?'

'What about Paul's thorn in the flesh? He had some eye disease didn't he?'

'My brother died when he was ill, so I lost my faith in God.'

'When hands were laid on me nothing happened. I didn't feel a thing.'

'I'm still waiting for my miracle.'

'Healing went out years ago. It's not for the church today.'

Chapter 1

WHY HASN'T GOD HEALED ME?

The answer to that is of course that He has, according to His Word, though many have not yet received the manifestation of their healing. Unless we have been taught the truth of the Bible, that Jesus died on the cross for our sins and our sickness, we have no foundation for this belief.

Because there is so much sickness in the church today, many church leaders are reluctant to teach that healing is available today for those who seek it, largely because action will be involved on someone's part. It also depends, of course, on what the leaders themselves have been taught, together as always with personal experiences.

The error has been in the translation of certain words in Isaiah chapter 53, which has led to contradictory interpretations of the truth. We always have to remember that the Bible is already a translation from the Hebrew and Greek languages and therefore open to shades of error, like any other translation. For instance, in Isaiah 53:4, the word **'griefs'** is more accurately translated **'sicknesses'**, i.e. physical illnesses. Certainly in the New King James version this word is cross-referenced with Matthew 8:17 (Strongs 769) to mean **'disease'** or **'sickness'**.

If we need further evidence, we see from Isaiah 52:14 where Jesus is described on the cross after crucifixion that **'His visage was marred more than any man and his form more than the sons of men'**. In other words, Jesus, disfigured by disease, could not be recognised as having been human at all. Hardly the normal appearance of someone after dying on the cross.

Isaiah verse 53 states **'And by his stripes we are healed'**. This definitely refers to physical healing as by a doctor (Strongs 7495). This interpretation is further confirmed by 1 Peter 2:24 where **'by whose stripes you were healed'** (Strongs 2390), the word 'healed' is translated 'cured'. Of course it is much easier to suggest that these words cover only spiritual healing, leaving no responsibility with us to search for anything more, but this does a huge disservice to Jesus who paid the price for it all.

Certainly, if we add the view that sickness was directly related to sin, as it was in the Old Testament and there is a connection today, if the sin has been paid for, what reason would there be for the sickness to remain? Under the law of cause and effect, it would be illogical for this to be so.

There is a danger in this association that those who are sick immediately take upon themselves the guilt of sin, and it is obvious why this is. I wish to stress however that there is no reason for a sick person to be under such condemnation. Sin can be involved somewhere, but it is not necessarily the sin of the sick person. It can have generational roots and come upon a person for many varied reasons of which they cannot be aware. Sick people who believe they deserve to be sick because of this should dispense with this thought immediately.

When we say that God is a loving God and could not possibly make us sick, people will immediately turn to examples in the Bible to disprove that truth. They may state that the Egyptians were inflicted with boils in Exodus 9:9 but this was surely one incident in a number of afflictions laid on them for which they received due warning. Job is another classic example of how God is supposed to bring misfortune upon His people, but it is overlooked that it was the devil who inflicted disease upon Job after he had sought permission from God.

The main example, however, which is most often quoted, is Paul's thorn. This was described by him as a 'messenger of Satan' in 2 Corinthians

12:7. The Greek word used is 'angelos', which is used throughout the Bible to mean a messenger in the form of a personality. The inference that Paul suffered from ophthalmia, an eye disease, comes from a mention in Galatians 4:15 of a suggestion that help would have been forthcoming from the disciples because of an isolated problem with his eyes, possibly, one might think, as a result of the many beatings and stonings he suffered throughout his apostleship.

Another reason given for sickness is that people say God has made them a better person through suffering and that He has used it to teach them something. If this is the case, implying that God wants us sick, what business have they going to a doctor for a cure? The logic is confusing. Jesus spent most of His working life healing people. If this was not God's will, why did He spend so much time in healing people? Indeed, in John 5:19 He says, **'Most assuredly I say to you, the Son can do nothing of Himself but what He sees the Father do; for whatever He does, the Son also does in like manner,'** proving God as the healer.

To completely trust God for our healing we must have a firm conviction of what He is like, His personality. All the information we need about God is contained in His Word and we can get to know Him through this by revelation of the Holy Spirit. It tells us who He is, what He has done and what His intentions are towards us. We know He describes Himself in the Old Testament as 'Jehovah Rapha', usually translated as God the Healer. 'Rapha' actually refers to restoration of any kind, to make whole or complete, so that first and foremost our God is a God of restoration.

As He is a covenant-making God, we know that He is honourable and faithful to keep His Word. Covenants, as we shall see later, carry a heavy responsibility for those making them and heavy penalties for those who break their terms. Deuteronomy 7:8 says **'but because the Lord loves you and because He would keep the oath which He swore to your fathers'**. We know also that He is a God of love and loving kindness and that He **'will withhold no good thing from those who walk uprightly'** (Psalm 84:1). Is healing a good thing?

We know that He is a God of loving kindness and mercy from Psalm 103:4, and this psalm again states that He heals all our diseases. Psalm 112, verse 4 tells us that **'He is gracious and full of compassion and righteousness'.** His Word tells us a good deal about the goodness of God.

Malachi 3:6 tells us that He never changes and Paul tells us in Romans 2:11 that there is **'no partiality with God'**. This means that we are all equal in His sight and no one gets preferential treatment. When Jesus was healing at the behest of His Father there is no record of His ever having refused to heal anyone who came to Him or ever having said it was not the right time for the person to be healed. **'He healed them all'** - Matthew 12:15 and Luke 6:19.

God's intention is always to bless us. Galatians 3:14 tells us that Christ died on the cross that the blessings of Abraham might come upon the Gentiles. Surely sickness can never be regarded as a blessing?

When we are agreed that God has no favourites, stated again by Peter in Acts 10:34, that He is willing to heal, and that healing is available to everyone who comes to Jesus as their Healer, we can begin to seriously consider ourselves as prospective candidates for healing. But if we think of God as someone fierce and unforgiving who is just waiting to punish us for our sins, as many do, then we have little chance of believing that we can receive healing from Him.

Why would a God who we imagine hates us sacrifice His only Son to restore us to the initial intimate relationship with Him, destroyed by Satan and Adam? We have to keep in mind the reason God created us in the first place. If it had been a careless act and it didn't matter if it went wrong, why was God so disappointed in the separation? However, if we really believe that God created us to fellowship with Him (Adam and Eve in the Garden) and that He was greatly upset when it all went wrong, we must give Him the benefit of the doubt in wanting to restore us to Him and put things right any way He could.

It is sad that His willingness to heal has not been matched by our willingness to receive from

Him. Many churches today are teaching that Jesus died on the cross only to reconcile us with God for our sin and choose to ignore the benefits of healing and prosperity. We have already seen that that is not what the Bible says. Their unwillingness to receive what God has provided is both ungracious and unscriptural, but a gift is not a gift until it is received. We can present a gift to a friend, beautifully wrapped, very expensive and put it on the table in front of them. It could still be there on the following birthday or Christmas, never having been received and never benefiting them at all. Many Christians leave their healing on the table!

Why would God want us sick when we could serve Him so much better in good health? To those beloved people with serious sickness or injury who say that God has used them to bring people to Him, I would point out that God will use any situation that we give Him to our advantage, but that it is not necessarily His best for us. He is so gracious that He will use us any way He can, but how much better it would be for them if they pursued and received their healing. I say 'pursue' because He is a **'rewarder of those who diligently seek Him** (Hebrews 11:6) Nevertheless, His best for us is voiced by John in 3 John 1, **'Beloved, I pray that you may prosper in all things and be in health, just as your soul prospers'**.

There will always be those who do not desperately want to be healed and are comfortable as they are. They may not want to take responsibility for themselves and their own lives and are very comfortable with their sickness. Unfortunately, it is unlikely that these people will admit to this state of affairs, so God is blamed for not healing them when it is not really what they want.

Yes, God is sovereign and can have His way at any point, but He prefers to give us a choice in the matter because He loves us and will not force us into anything. The choice is always ours to go after what He has provided for us. Deuteronomy 30:19 says, **'...therefore choose life, that both you and your descendants may live'**.

Chapter 2

WHAT IS A COVENANT, AND HOW DOES IT AFFECT MY HEALING?

If I were to ask people what an Old Testament covenant was they would probably say a kind of contract or agreement. But a covenant was much more than that and not as easily got out of as some contracts are today. It was more of a pact, a guarantee of support and services, to get people onside, to share their strengths and help cover their weaknesses. Covenants were about relationship.

The word 'covenant' actually means ' to cut where blood flows'. Circumcision was a covenant and marriage is a covenant, confirmed when the bride is a virgin. Biblical covenants were made to access the strengths of the other party and to get them to cover your weaknesses. It is reported that the pioneering explorer David Livingstone survived so well in Africa by making covenants with all the tribes he encountered. This meant that they would have to stand by him in the event of an attack. It would also make any potential attacker cautious, as they would have no way of knowing who he was in covenant with.

To make a covenant, both sides would have to be in agreement concerning their obligations. Say, for an unlikely example, we have two tribes named Smith and Jones. The Smiths were experts with the spear but useless at close-quarter combat. So, whilst they were excellent hunters and ate very well they suffered greatly from attackers who were better fighters than they were. The Jones tribe were skilled swordsmen and experts in warfare. Unfortunately they were not so good at killing game for their food. Both tribes had skills that the other needed so they would make a covenant together in full view of witnesses and mutual agreement of both tribes. This would last for at least eight generations and any individual who broke a covenant would be hunted down and killed by either side, even his own family. So we see that covenants were a serious business.

Incidentally, another word for 'covenant' is 'testament'. God made several with His people in the Old Testament, firstly with Noah in Genesis 9:11 concerning the flood and again with Abram in Genesis 15:8 when He gave them the Promised Land. But the covenant which concerns us most here is what is known as the Healing Covenant made with Moses when God declared Himself as 'Jehovah Rapha', our Healer. It is important to note here that this promise of healing was conditional upon the obedience of the people to God's Laws and His Voice.

Exodus 15:26 says **'If you diligently heed the voice of the Lord your God and do what is right in His sight, give ear to His commandments and keep all His statutes, I will put (allow) none of the diseases on you that I have brought (allowed) on the Egyptians. For I am the Lord who heals you'.** Deuteronomy 7:9 says, **'He is God, the faithful God who keeps covenant and mercy for a thousand generations with those who love Him and keep His commandments'.** Verse 15 says, **'And the Lord will take away from you all sickness'.** Does this apply to us today? Yes it does, because Deuteronomy 29:14 says, **'I make this covenant and this oath, not with you alone** [verse 15], **but with him who stands here with us today before the Lord our God, as well as with him who is not here with us today'** (i.e. future generations). Did God keep this covenant? Yes He did.

There was no sickness amongst the Israelites while they were obedient to God. Psalm 105:37 says, **'He brought them forth (from Egypt)**

also with silver and gold and there was not one feeble person among their tribes'. In Deuteronomy 9:5 Moses says, **'And I have led you forty years in the wilderness. Your clothes have not worn out on you and your sandals have not worn out on your feet'**. So we note that God takes covenants seriously.

There was always a covenant ceremony which was formally enacted when all the members of both tribes were present and a feast was held. Firstly, animals were ritually sacrificed and the two halves laid on the ground. There was always a great deal of blood. The two tribal chiefs then walked a figure of eight between them. They then exchanged weapons - this signified 'my enemies are now your enemies' and vice versa. Anyone attacking one may be considered as attacking the other.

The two chieftains then exchanged cloaks and headgear which said 'my rank is now your rank and my authority is now your authority', meaning 'my men are now at your disposal. Your debts, responsibilities and liabilities are now mine'. Wrists were then ceremonially cut and bound together to signify the oneness of both families or tribes. The wounds were not allowed to heal but were rubbed with salt in order to leave a permanent scar on the wrist. Our own hand-shaking ceremony was originally created to show whether covenant scars existed on the person being greeted. Likewise the familiar Red Indian greeting of 'How!' with a raised hand was to show covenant scars to intimidate a possible enemy. We have all heard of blood brothers. Lastly, tribal names were exchanged and the tribe would be known as the Smith-Jones tribe. As with the wedding breakfast, this was celebrated with a feast.

Why do we need to know these details of covenant making? To show God's sincere intentions towards His people. To indicate His intention for His people to remain free from sickness, God made the covenant with Himself (Gen 22:16) **'By Myself have I sworn said the Lord.'** It was because Abram appeared dubious that God went to these lengths. **'Lord God, whereby shall I know that I shall inherit it?'** When God called for sacrificial animals, Abram knew that He had a covenant in mind. In Genesis verse 17 a smoking oven and a burning torch passed between those pieces.

Taking the 'ah' from Jahweh (Jehovah), Abram's name was changed to Abraham. Verse 6 says that Abram believed in the Lord and it was accounted to him for righteousness, an important relationship word. We have no reason to believe that God was in any way less serious about His healing covenant.

However, it became obvious to God over a period of time that it was impossible for the Israelites to maintain their obedience to Him and as this was necessary to maintain the covenant, God was unable to do His part in maintaining their healing. Therefore, a new plan was required and this came in the form of a New Covenant introduced by Jesus. He spoke of this in the upper room at the Last Supper, announcing it when He took the cup of wine and gave it to them saying, **'Drink from it, all of you. For this is my blood of the new covenant which is shed for many for the remission of sins'. Hebrews 12:24 calls Jesus 'the mediator of a new covenant'.**

It follows that the new covenant would not be as difficult to keep as the old, which was so easily broken. Hebrews 8:6 says, **'But now He has obtained a more excellent ministry, inasmuch as He is also Mediator of a better covenant which was established on better promises. For if that first covenant had been faultless, then no place would have been sought for a second'**. In other words, we get a better deal with the new covenant which makes it easier for God to provide for our healing because the conditions are nowhere near as stringent.

The exchange of cloaks came about when Jesus took upon Himself our sin, sickness and poverty and in exchange gave us His robe of righteousness: **'For He has clothed me with the garments of salvation, He has covered me with the robe of righteousness** (this is **important to our healing'.** 1 Peter 2:24 says, **'who Himself bore our sins in His own body on the tree. As to the exchange of weapons, we had no weapons against the devil until Ephesians 6:11 invites us to 'put on the whole armour of God.'** We also have the authority that Jesus gave us after His death and we must not overlook 'the sword of the spirit' which is the Word of God.

When Jesus died on the cross, the covenant ceremony was re-enacted in full. Until then, on the Day of Atonement each year the priest had entered the holy of holies in the temple and sprinkled the blood of sacrificed animals on the mercy seat. (Leviticus chapter 16) This was to make atonement for all the uncleanness of the children of Israel and for all their transgressions and sins. In this way all sins were covered from the sight of God. It is interesting to note that as soon as Adam and Eve realised their nakedness, **'The Lord God made for them tunics of skin and clothed them'** (Gen. 3:21).

Also as part of the atonement, the priest would lay his hands on the chosen scapegoat (in this case a real goat) and confess over it all the iniquities of the children of Israel. The scapegoat would then be released into the wilderness, carrying away all their sin. (Lev.16:22)

The New Covenant provided for us by Jesus

also dealt with the whole of our sins and sickness, past present and future, and removed them from us **'As far as the east is from the west'** (Psalm 103:12). This made the provision for us that God would not view them in the same way as sins committed under the Law, which had been impossible to keep. This is conditional, of course, on our recognising what Jesus has done and on our being repentant of any sin committed. The stipulation that Jesus made during His lifetime was that we wholly love God and that we walk in love and forgiveness toward one another. Through Jesus' sacrifice on the cross, we have been made righteous in the sight of God.

The blood of sacrificed animals was poured out by Jesus in Luke 22:20: **'This cup is the new covenant in my blood which is shed for you'**. The covenant was cut when one of the soldiers pierced His side with a spear and immediately blood and water came out (John 19:34). Names changed when believers, first of all in Antioch, became known as Christ-ians or 'little anointed ones'.

Holy Communion can be taken as a re-enactment of the covenant ceremony of the Last Supper and many people have been healed when regarding the bread as the body of Christ. Healing under the New Covenant is readily available to all who come to Jesus as the provider of their healing. If we have sinned, God will no longer count these sins against us, if we repent, because we have been made righteous or sinless, by the blood of Jesus.

Chapter 3

IF NOT FROM GOD, WHERE DOES SICKNESS COME FROM?

If God does not want us sick, where does sickness come from? Did God create sickness?

We have to go back to Genesis 1, verses 10, 12, 17, 21 and 25 which state that, regarding His creation, **'God saw that it was good'**. Verse 31 says **'Then God saw everything that He had made and indeed it was very good'**. How can it be regarded as very good when sickness was allowed to happen to the Israelites as a reward for disobedience? God obviously does not consider there is any good in sickness and it follows that His best for us is that we never get sick in the first place.

God said, **'Let us make man in our image'** (Strongs 6754, meaning 'a representative figure'). Surely a true likeness of God would not include any predisposition towards sickness of any kind. God is a God of light and life, not of sickness and disease. The tree of life was in the Garden of Eden and God created man with endless human life to fellowship with Him endlessly. But the tree of the knowledge of good and evil was also there and this was the tree they were told not to eat from (Genesis 2:16), or they would surely die. This refers to spiritual death or separation from God. We must remember that God is a Spirit and does not exist as we do in physical terms.

Everything was going well until along came Satan, who wanted the worship and adoration belonging to God for himself. Isaiah 14:12 tells us that he said, **'I will be like the most high'**. This is a familiar stance, reminding us that he also said to Jesus, **'All these things I will give you if thou wilt fall down and worship me'** (Matthew 4:9).

Satan immediately set about destroying Adam's faith in the Word of God, **'Has God indeed said...?'** and he is still doing it today. He told them, 'You will not surely die... you will be like God knowing good and evil' (Genesis 3:5). Adam was responsible and should not have eaten the fruit, but he did and subsequently hid from God. We know the consequences only too well. In Genesis 1:26 Adam had been given dominion over the earth, but he lost this when he obeyed Satan instead of God. His dominion rested on his obedience to God. So Adam became separated from God and therefore spiritually dead. There was no spirit life in his body to indefinitely maintain physical life and his body died when he was 930 years old (Genesis 5:5). This confirms that healing begins when we begin to maintain the life of our spirits and our relationship with God. Physical death is the separation of the spirit from the body. Before we get too discouraged, however, we should remember that God is gracious and merciful and that there is no situation, I repeat no situation, from which we cannot recover and receive our healing.

Does this mean then that everyone who is sick is in some sort of sin? No, it does not. We have discovered that sickness entered the world through sin, and sin may be involved somewhere, but not necessarily with the sick person, and it is wrong to place guilt upon sick people as is often done. We shall discuss this further later on.

In Romans 5:19, Paul says **'For as by one man's disobedience many were made sinners, so also by one Man's obedience many will be made righteous'**. Here Paul is referring to Jesus' death on the cross, which fully restored our relationship with God and the damage done by Adam's sin. The fact that sickness and death came through sin was fully acknowledged in Jesus' time and certainly confirmed by Him because Jesus worked in this environment. John 9:3 says, **'Rabbi, who sinned, this man or his parents that he was born blind?'** John 5:14 says, **'Afterwards Jesus found him in the temple**

and said to him, 'See you have been made well. Sin no more lest a worse thing come upon you.' Luke 5:23 says, **'Which is easier to say, your sins be forgiven or to say rise up and walk.'** It is important to note here that this was BEFORE Jesus had died on the cross.

In the Old Testament, on the Day of Atonement each year the priest would make sacrifice for the sins of the people. When Jesus died He became the once for all sacrifice for all our sins past and present and wiped the slate clean. Psalm 103:12 says, **'As far as the East is from the West, so far has He removed our transgression from us'**. John 1:9 says, **'If we confess our sins, He is faithful and just to forgive us our sins and to cleanse us from all unrighteousness'**. Romans 8:2 says, **'For the Law of the Spirit of Life has made us free from the law of sin and death'**, which was recognised in Jesus' day. It follows that WE CANNOT BE OPERATING UNDER BOTH LAWS AT THE SAME TIME. God has given us a choice.

John 10:10 records Jesus as saying of the devil, **'The thief does not come except to steal, and to kill, and to destroy. I have come that they may have life and have it more abundantly'**, i.e. without sickness, which He proved by His ministry of healing.

So we know how sin, sickness and disease originated, but what are the causes of sickness? What gives the devil the right to put sickness on us?

1) Unrepented sin, which is disobedience of the Word of God as indicated by Jesus.

2) Self-induced sickness caused by self-indulgence such as overeating, drug or alcohol abuse and generally misusing our bodies.

   These diseases of cause and effect are mainly due to temptation and we may need the help of the Holy Spirit to overcome them. But rest assured, there is nothing that cannot be overcome.

3) Generational and other curses

Because we have been made righteous and sinless through Jesus, it follows that any sin marring our relationship with a loving and forgiving God must have arisen through our disobedience or just plain ignorance. It is possible for sin of which we are unaware to influence our lives when it has been put there by someone else. Nevertheless it is just as effective in its influence. Because we are unaware of these occurrences we are not exempt from the influence they can have, because ignorance is not a valid plea. Even unintentional sin had to be accounted for and the requisite atonement made (Numbers 15:24-29).

How then can others place a sin influence on our lives? There are many possibilities. They can curse us with words which, if we take them to heart and possibly repeat them, can have a real and sometimes lasting influence on our lives. For instance, when friends, parents or teachers speak negatively over us, they can place us outside of God's vision for us, which is not scriptural. If we adopt these sayings, e.g. 'You'll never amount to much, you always make a mess of things, you'll never be any good at that', we can fall into negative thinking and behaviour patterns and thereby miss God's best for us. We must never forget how much God loves us and wants a fruitful and successful life for each of us. By adopting negative thoughts and actions which are lies, we are giving the devil authority over our lives to **'steal and kill and destroy'**, which is his main aim in life (John 10:10).

Our ancestors can unknowingly play a large part in our Christian lives if they have been into idolatry, witchcraft or any kind of ungodly pursuit which has influenced the way they behaved towards God. These occurrences can allow evil spirits to come down the generational line and manifest themselves somehow in a later family. Very often, people with strong addictions to things like alcohol, tobacco or pornography find they are unable to overcome their weaknesses without spiritual help. Because these spirits have not been separated or 'cast out' from the family line they can influence future generations, sometimes skipping a generation. These spirits are recognised in the Old Testament as 'familiar spirits' and are not to be feared as they are easily dealt with through the blood of Jesus and can be cut off - a wise move, whether they are known to be present or simply suspected. When, according to the Bible, three or four generations are involved (Exodus 20:5), and we cannot possibly know all that they have been up to, it is safest to have a 'spring clean' anyway.

If we are not sure where our problems or sickness are coming from, we can ask the Holy Spirit to show us and, with perseverance, we will eventually find the cause. It is not in God's interests for us to remain sick when we can do so much more for the kingdom of God when we are fit and well.

In place of the old Law with all its complications, Jesus gave us a new ruling. John 3:13 says, **'A new commandment I give to you that you love one another, as I have loved you; that you also love one another'**. Verse 35 says, **'By this all will know that you are my disciples if you have love one for another.'** It is important that we realise that we are unlikely to receive the manifestation of our healing if we are not walking in agape love towards all of our brothers and sisters'.

Because Jesus performed so many miracles, it has become more or less standard to expect miraculous healings, but this is often not the case. We shall see later when we discuss how we believe the power of God works that healing is often gradual. The incident that most people will quote when we mention gradual healing is when Jesus' power appeared to falter. With the man who said, **'I see men like trees walking'** (Mark 8:24), Jesus then had to touch him again, and this has somehow given the impression that gradual healing is not the real thing. Therefore many people write off their healing if they do not experience an instant miracle and many healings are lost in this way. Many people believe that they are walking in faith for their healing by constantly saying year after year that they are 'believing' for their healing and that 'God is going to heal them'. Unfortunately, these people have not had any real teaching about faith, have not believed that their healing was instigated by God when they prayed, and many have died, still confessing that God was 'going to heal them'.

Because of the number of anointed people of God who minister healing, it is sometimes difficult to assess why some healings appear to take place and some do not. It may seem as though there are no rules and that God is somehow haphazard in bestowing healing or is having a 'bad hair day'. Whilst the anointing of God is not to be belittled in any way, certainly Jesus ministered entirely under it, a very real knowledge of God and His Word are no less valid in producing healing today. It is easy to say that God is sovereign and that there are no ground rules attached to healing but we know from convention reports etc. that many who appear healed are later seen to lose their healing. What I am trying to say here is that the Word of God is far safer than any report or experience when people are seeking to be healed.

If we believe in a loving God who is faithful and gave us His Word so that we should understand what He requires of us, it would be unreasonable to suggest that He has not given us all the answers that we need. There are, of course, mysteries we shall not be privileged to understand, but these are surely far more scattered than some would have us believe. It is also impossible for Him to go against His Word without providing a massive opening for an attack from Satan. So we can confidently believe in a God who has set down rules and standards for us to live by in order to receive full blessings from Him.

People continually say, 'Not everyone gets healed'. Whilst this is true according to our observation, not everyone gets saved, although salvation, we are told, is available to all. Otherwise we would have to accept that Jesus did not die for everyone and that God is, after all, 'a respecter of persons', which the Bible clearly tells us He is not (Acts 10:34). Unfortunately some churches teach that when we are 'born again' i.e. when we give our lives to Jesus, salvation and healing are automatic and there is no more to be done. Whilst we are spiritually saved, our minds and emotions are not renewed to God and it does not follow that we are immediate candidates for all His benefits. Nor does it follow that all sin has been expiated and repented of, so we cannot possibly be automatic candidates for instant healing. It is true healing exists for us, but we have to appropriate it by doing whatever God requires of us.

In his description of the 4th Dimension, David Yonggi Cho paints a picture of a place where our blessings exist for us, just waiting to be brought into existence by our prayer, speech or action. This places the responsibility of the degree of blessing we receive squarely on us. Many people are waiting on blessings just falling out of the sky, but the Bible indicates that this is not how it works. **'God is a rewarder of those who diligently seek Him'** (Hebrews 11:6) and we must never forget that.

Andrew Wommack, in his wonderful teaching in a CD series called 'God Wants You Well', tells us that the way we deal with any delay between praying for the manifestation of our healing and actually seeing something happen is important. It is so important to stick to our guns and not be led astray by doubt and unbelief and any temptation to voice doubts about our healing. In this way our faith is maintained as a powerful force and will act with the Word of God to produce the desired result.

We have seen that God did not create sickness. Jesus told His disciples to preach the kingdom of God and heal the sick. Surely this again indicates that there is no sickness in the kingdom of God and it did not originate from there. To those who adamantly preach and teach that Jesus death on the cross did not release us from sickness and disease it can only be said that if they only preach half the benefits of the atonement, half the benefits is all they can expect.

Chapter 4

THE WORD OF GOD, AND WHAT IT TELLS US ABOUT HEALING

Apart from the Holy Spirit within us, the Bible or Word of God is the only true source of the knowledge of God. It tells us what He is like, what He expects of us and what we can expect of Him. Everything began with the Word and God means us to make use of it today. John 1:1-3 says, **'In the beginning was the Word and the Word was God. He (Jesus) was in the beginning with**

God. All things were made by Him and without Him nothing was made that was made.'

It is difficult for us today to realise the power of the Word of God when we are surrounded by words of every shape and size in books and newspapers and from radio, TV and each other. We are constantly bombarded by words. However, they do not have the power to create in the same way that God's Word does. It never fails to amaze me that as children we easily accept the power of witches and their spells, but we can have problems in realising that God creates with words. That's His way, and it has to become our way if we want to succeed.

Let's look at the creativity of God's Word. The world was created by God's speaking it into existence with faith-filled words. Genesis contains the history of creation and in the first 31 verses 'God said' occurs 15 times. Hebrews 1:3 tells us God is **'upholding all things by the word of his power.'** God also said 'let us make man in our image', making our words creative too, but more of that later.

We know from the Bible that His Word is not like any other. In Hebrew 4:12, Paul tells us that it is **'living and powerful, and sharper than any two-edged sword, piercing even to the division of soul and spirit, and of joints and marrow, and is a discerner of the thoughts and intents of the heart'** (powerful in the sense that it contains 'dunamis' or miracle-working power). Ephesians 6:14 tells us to take the sword of the Spirit, which is the Word of God'. This is the only offensive weapon we have against the devil.

God regards His Word very seriously. Psalm 138:2 says, **'For You have magnified Your Word above all Your name'.** What does He say about it? **'For as the rain comes down and the snow from heaven and do not return there, But water the earth and make it bring forth and bud, That it may give seed to the sower and bread to the eater, So shall My Word be that goes forth from my mouth; It shall not return to Me void, But it shall accomplish what I please, And it shall prosper in the thing for which I sent it'.** We know that Psalm

107:20 says, **'He sent His Word and healed them'**, making God's Word and Jesus and healing all interchangeable in that context.

We are told in Romans 10:17 that God's Word has the power to develop our faith. The ordinary written Word of the Bible, the Logos, can be turned into a Rhema or revelation word revealed to our spirits. When we have this kind of revelation about its meaning, the Word can work powerful things in our lives. But the Word cannot be revealed to our spirits if we have not made ourselves familiar with it in the first place. In Joshua 1:8, God tells him to **'meditate in it day and night, that you may observe to do all that is written in it. For then you will make your way prosperous and then you will have good success'.** The interesting thing about the word 'meditate' is that in this context it means to 'mutter'. Note, the Word must not depart from Joshua's mouth and he is to keep repeating it to himself.

John 17:17 says, **'Your Word is truth'**. Facts and circumstances may change but God's Word will never change. He is His Word. Numbers 23:19

says, **'God is not a man that He should lie, Nor a son of man that He should repent, i.e. change his mind. Has He not said, and will He not do?'**

The devil's job is to make God out to be a liar and nullify His Word. If the devil can steal the word from us he will rob us of our most powerful weapon. In John 8:44, Jesus is speaking about this to the Pharisees. **'Ye are of your father the devil, and the desires of your father you want to do. He was a murderer from the beginning, and does not stand in the truth, because there is no truth in him. When he speaks a lie, he speaks from his own resources, for he is a liar and the father of it.'**

1 Thessalonians 2:13 says, **'when you received the word of God which you heard from us, you welcomed it not as the word of man, but as it is in truth, the Word of God... which also effectively works in you who believe.'** We have to receive God's Word as the truth. 2 Timothy 2:15 says, **'Be diligent to present yourself approved of God, a worker who does not need to be ashamed rightly**

dividing (discerning) the Word of truth.' In John 8:32 **'...and you shall know the truth and the truth shall set you free.'**

God's Word contains all that we need because it contains **'all that pertains to life and godliness'** (1Peter 1:3). Whatever problems we have, the answer will be found in the Word. But does it contain healing power? Psalm 107:20: **'He sent His Word and healed them.'** God says it does. In Proverbs 4, verses 20-24 He says, **'My son, give attention to my words; Incline your ear to my sayings, Do not let them depart from your eyes, Keep them in the midst of your heart; For they are life to those who find them, and health to all their flesh'**. In John 1:1 it is called the Word of life.

Kenneth Hagin tells of a woman who had not worn normal shoes all her life because of the lack of a little toe on one foot. All she did was to bury herself in the Word of God by listening to an audio tape, and after six months the toe grew.

I like what Joyce Myer says: ' Jesus can heal you everywhere you hurt.'

Chapter 5

WHAT ARE YOU SAYING ABOUT YOUR SICKNESS?

Actually, it's very wrong of me to call it 'your sickness' because it does not belong to you unless you own it. If you believe, as I do, that Jesus took all our sin and sickness upon Himself, there is absolutely no need for us to suffer as He did. It has all been dealt with.

Charles Capps tells us in his book, 'The Tongue - A Creative Force' that Jesus said, 'I have told my people they can have what they say, but they are saying what they have' and this is certainly true of sickness in the church today. We are all too ready to describe what we see and ensure that every detail and symptom of sickness is mentioned - sometimes to gain maximum sympathy from enquirers.

There is enormous power in what we say, and all words are tremendously powerful because they are creative. How can I say that? Firstly, we have to remember that our God creates things with words and this is difficult for people to grasp. If you ask people what they think, they often imagine God hard at work with a heap of clay or stare at you blankly. We have seen, however, that God spoke the world into being (Genesis 1:26).

It is also important that we grasp that God said **'Let us make man in our image according to our likeness'**, which in translation (Strongs 6754) means patterned on the specifications from which an actual item is made'. We are made exactly in God's image. This surely means that we have every right to expect that our words are creative too and therefore we, like God, will have what we say. This includes healing. God tells us to pay attention to His words, they are health to all our flesh. All we have to do is agree with them and repeat them.

God Himself recognised the power of what we say even if we do not. If you will recall what happened with the Tower of Babel in Genesis 11, God said **'with one language, nothing they propose to do will be withheld from them'** (verse 6). What we say is that powerful! In order to destroy their power God had to confuse their language so that they no longer understood one another. Remember also that God told Joshua to keep the Word in his mouth and to mutter it.

Jesus told us in Mark 11:23 how to deal with the mountain of sickness, **'For assuredly, I say to you, whoever says to this mountain, Be removed and be cast into the sea, and does not doubt in his heart, but believes that those things he says will be done, he will have whatever he says.'** In effect, Jesus is saying we can have whatever we say. Not what we think about, not what we pray, but what we SAY. We must thank God before we see the manifestation of what we want to happen because **'God calls those things that did not exist as though they did'** (Romans 4:17). We should not be speaking what we see, but what we want to see.

Proverbs 18:21 says, **'Death and life are in the power of the tongue'.** In Deuteronomy, God tells us to choose life. How do we choose life? We speak it. We have to realise that we are a product of what either we or someone else has spoken over our lives.

It is well known by psychiatrists that the part of the brain that controls our speech also influences our bodily action. Dr Paul Yonggi Cho says in volume 2 of *The Fourth Dimension,* 'The speech centre in the brain has direct influence over the entire nervous system'. Also, 'The recovery of a patient and the ability to stay alive is contained in the patient's will, which is affected by what the patient confesses.' This means that whatever we say about our sickness will also be picked up on by bodily action and the body will quite naturally fall in with whatever the mouth has spoken to the brain. Consequently if we say, 'I think it's getting worse', we can see what the brain and body's reaction will be. God has made us so wonderfully that everything we need is contained within us. The only addition we need is the presence of the Holy Spirit when we are born again to make us complete in His sight. Particularly as we get older, we must take care not to adopt society's view of our situation and let ourselves be put into categories that are not godly, e.g. that we must expect certain illnesses as we get older.

Jesus said in Matthew 15:11, **'Not what goes into the mouth defiles a man; but what comes out of the mouth, this defiles a man'**, ...verse 18, 'those things which proceed out of the mouth come from the heart, and they defile a man.

Since Jesus is the High Priest of our confession (Hebrews 3:1) who **'always lives to make intercession for us** (Hebrews 7:25)**, seated at God's right hand'** (Hebrews 8:1) so that through

Him we may have what agrees with the Word of God because, **'No good thing will He withhold from those who walk uprightly'** (Psalm 84:11). Proverbs 21:23 says, **'He who guards his mouth and his tongue keeps himself from calamity'**. All these instructions are to warn us that we must be very careful what we say. It is useless saying positive things about our healing and quoting the Word of God if we interject with destructive words, even as a joke.

'Sticks and stones may break my bones but words will never hurt me' could not be further from the truth. We can curse ourselves or let other people do it for us, but as we have already seen, if we mentally take a thought on board so that it becomes a magnified possibility, it will go to work in our lives. 'I don't think I'll ever get over this', 'It's got to get worse before it gets better,' or a friend saying, 'you'll never...' can all do destructive harm to our healing and we should repent of such sayings or of taking anything similar on board if we want the Word and only the Word to work in our lives. Any words can be powerful and they are also a means of letting the devil know what is really going on in our hearts, thereby giving him an opening to instill doubt and unbelief in our minds.

We have to copy God and **'call those things that are not as though they were'** (Romans 4:17) until we see the manifestation of our healing. This is the way God works. **'By faith we understand that the worlds were framed by the Word of God, so the things which are seen were not made of things which are visible'** (Hebrews 11:3).

When people ask us how we are, we can be all too ready to describe our symptoms in detail and say how we feel. The devil delights in putting symptoms on us, but they are only symptoms until we give them a name. When we speak about sickness, we are giving it life and glorifying the works of the devil. SYMPTOMS ARE NOT A DISEASE UNTIL WE TURN THEM INTO ONE BY ACCEPTING THEM AS FORERUNNERS OF SICKNESS. The kind of thing we say is, 'I've got a sore throat, I think I am getting a cold' - if that is what you believe, rest assured that you will! If we can ignore symptoms, they will go away because we have not given them any authority to stay. Proverbs 6:2 says, **'You are snared by the words of your mouth'**.

James 3:3-12 describes the damage that we can do by thoughtless and ungodly speech. **'Even so the tongue is a little member and boasts great things. See how great a forest a little fire kindles! But no man can tame the tongue. It is an unruly evil, full of deadly poison.'**

Whenever people ask us how we are, we should reply by saying something like, 'healed and whole in the name of Jesus'. I sometimes think that when people have been prayed for it would be a good idea to supply a large piece of sticking plaster over the mouth to stop them from destroying the healing power before it has had any chance to work. Jesus told us to speak TO the mountain, not ABOUT it. We should command the sickness to leave and then keep quiet about it. If we continue to confess sickness we shall be holding onto it and the Word of God cannot help us, as happens when we cease to agree with His Word, God can do nothing.

Matthew 12:36 reports Jesus as saying: **'But I tell you that men will have to give an account on the day of judgement for every careless word they have spoken'**. 'Careless' here is translated as not agreeing with the Word of God. These are idle or insincere words that we are all guilty of, e.g. 'I'm dying for a cup of tea... I expect I'll have the flu, I get it every year at about this time... I'm sure to have an accident if I...'

Matthew 5:37 says, **'Simply let your 'yes' be 'yes' and your 'no' be 'no'. Anything beyond this comes from the evil one.' In other words, 'If you don't mean it, don't say it'.**

This is easy to say, and most of us are guilty of having moments when we let our tongues run away with us. James 3:8 says, '**But no man can tame the tongue. It is an unruly evil full of deadly poison'**. Most Christians have no idea of the importance of what they say and how it affects their lives. This seems to be mainly because of lack of teaching. Hosea 4:6 says, **'My people are**

destroyed through lack of knowledge,' and this was never truer than it is of the church today when we consider the amount of sickness and the number of early deaths it is carrying.

1 Peter 2:24 tells us, **'by whose stripes you were healed'**. If we were healed, then we are healed and we should never again confess sickness. If we do not see an immediate miracle, at least we have sown the seed for one to take place. In Mark 4:14, Jesus tells us that the Word of God is a seed and therefore it will operate under the law of seedtime and harvest. Genesis 8:22 says, **'While the earth remains, seedtime and harvest, Cold and heat, Winter and summer, And day and night shall not cease.'** Seedtime and harvest is an unchanging law of the universe. Seeds produce after their own kind, and so do words.

When we sow seeds we are not in the practice of digging them up every day to see how they are doing. We use our faith to believe that things are happening underground, and although we cannot see it we believe that underground growth is taking place. In the same way we must believe for our healing and that the process is taking place towards its manifestation, although we may not see it, or quite the opposite may seem to be happening. We have sown the seed to set it in motion and must believe for a successful harvest.

If we have not adequately prepared the ground, i.e. the Word of God has not been sufficiently planted in us so that we can believe without doubt that God has already healed us, we need to 'go back to the drawing board' and change our circumstances. Certainly the Word itself and the promises of God will not change.

In Mark 4:26, Jesus says, **'The kingdom of God is as if a man should scatter seed upon the ground.'** There is a set process at work and words are process starters. The Word of God will grow and produce in our lives - seedtime and harvest is operated by us to bring into our lives what we say. We must repent of any idle words we have spoken which can nullify the effect of God's Word.

We must learn to speak the answer and not the problem. We must learn to say, like Smith

Wigglesworth, 'I am not moved by what I see but by what the Word of God says about me.' We can create our own futures by what we speak into our lives, positive or negative words. Charles Capps recommends that we regularly repeat the Word of God throughout the day when the devil is attempting to put sickness on us. In this way what we say will come to pass as it is created by our speech and the sickness will have no means by which to stay. If we will not accept symptoms, they cannot have authority to stay in our lives and will have to disappear.

Where the Spirit of the Lord is, there is freedom. We are free to accept or reject the doctor's diagnosis and replace it with the Word of God. We do not have to accept what other people say. We may see symptoms of sickness but we don't have to speak of them or own them. This may sound simple but of course it may take a little time. But the Word of God is faithful to work in us if we give it the opportunity, and sickness will become a thing of the past.

Chapter 6

WHAT DO YOU BELIEVE, I MEAN REALLY BELIEVE, ABOUT YOUR HEALING?

What we really believe in our hearts about our healing will determine whether or not we receive and keep our healing. Against all the odds such as what we see, what we are told, what we imagine, only faith in God as our healer through Jesus Christ will get the job done. The Bible says that without faith it is impossible to please God (Hebrews 11:6). Not unlikely, but impossible.

We must all have faith to be saved, given to us by God. **'For by grace you have been saved through faith, and that not of yourselves; it is the gift of God'**. Romans 12:3 says that God has dealt to each of us a measure of faith. **'It is up to each of us to develop that faith if we are to receive more from God'**. Jesus said on several occasions to those coming for healing, **'Your faith has made you whole'.** So it seems that faith is vital if we are to receive from God. The question is, how do we get it?

Romans 10:17 tells us that **'faith comes by hearing, and hearing by the word of God'**. This seems to imply that it is not just listening to the Word but hearing it with our 'spirit' ears, a special kind of hearing, as implied by Jesus in Luke 8:8 and Luke 14:35, Mark 7:16 and Matthew 11:15. This is because there are two kinds of knowledge, Sense Knowledge and Heart Knowledge. Sense or Head knowledge that comes from the senses is stored from what we see, hear, feel, taste, touch and smell. This means that although we know its potential, we can listen to the Logos or written word of God without its affecting our faith. In a way, it can bounce off without having any affect.

When it penetrates to our hearts to create faith, it is known as the Rhema or revealed word of God and it continually works in us, as described by Paul in 1 Thessalonians 2:13, to strengthen our faith. It is meditation on the word that brings faith, not the listening to. People will go to lecture after lecture

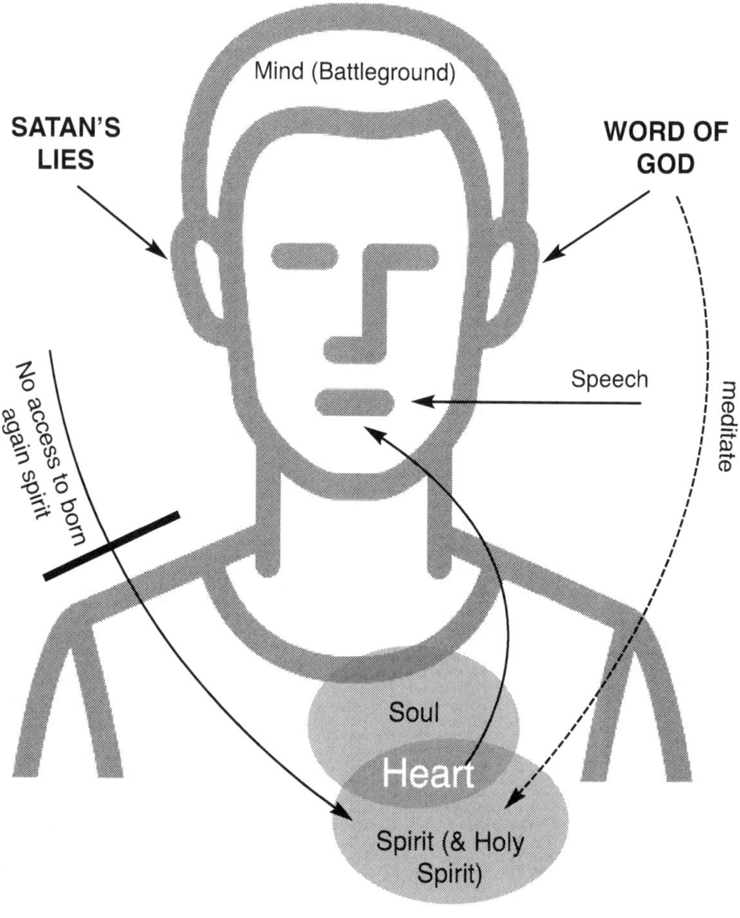

and meeting after meeting, and read every new book that is published but can end up with no more powerful a faith than they started with

We must have faith in God's Word because of who He is and what we know of His character. If we just have head knowledge of the Word, our faith can easily disappear when we see something happen which is not in line with what it says. We can lose confidence in it. We must have faith in a faithful God and not doubt that His Word means what it says. Real faith in God to keep His Word never changes, whatever the circumstances.

How do we know that our faith is real? When we are not afraid to act upon it. James, the brother of Jesus, explains that faith must have action. James 2:14 says, **'What does it profit, my brethren, if someone says he has faith but does not have works? Can faith save him?** [Verse 26] **For as the body without spirit is dead, so faith without works is dead also.'**

Smith Wigglesworth is reported to have said repeatedly, 'Faith is an act.' It is something that we do. People will say they have faith, but unless it prompts them to act it is not working for them. It is not quickened. Real faith can be seen in a person's actions, otherwise it lies dormant and cannot accomplish anything. When we act on our faith, it draws upon the power of God. In Mark 5:27 we notice the faith of the woman with the issue of blood: **'When she heard about Jesus'**, her faith was quickened **'for she said** [The Greek perfect continuous tense, ie she kept on saying] **if only I may touch His clothes, I shall be made well.'**

Her faith drew on the power of God. SHE instigated her healing through her faith. God will always hold fast to His Word and she had fulfilled the requirements to receive from Him. Jesus was aware of power leaving Him but He did not engineer her healing – she did. It is very comforting to know that if we follow the guidelines of the Word of God, what it says must take place.

My personal experience has been that when I have made an act of faith, however small, in expecting to receive from God, it has been rewarded. I recall that when I first became a Christian I had lost my job and was left with debts which, on the face of it, I had no hope of repaying. I was discussing this with a woman at my church who asked me 'Do you tithe?' meaning do you give one tenth of your income to the church, as suggested in the book of Malachi, Chapter 3. I said that I did because tithing and giving were regularly preached at the church. 'Then you don't have a problem,' she replied, 'Give it to God and let Him sort it out.' Being a new Christian and tending to believe what I was told before doubt and unbelief had time to set in, I decided to do just that. But how to show faith in my belief? Well I simply put all the bills etc. together and showed them to God, saying that I had been told He would take care of them, and left it at that.

Less than three weeks later, another woman from the church approached me and said that she had come into some money. I said how pleased I was for her, but she told me that I had missed the point and that God had told her to settle all my debts. After my first 'goldfish' reaction I was concerned that she did not know how much money was involved, but she was not the least concerned.

'God knows,' she said, 'just give me a total and I'll write you a cheque.' Resisting the devil's prompting to add just a little for good measure, I gave her the total of the faith package and she wrote me a cheque without a second glance saying, 'Don't thank me – thank God.' I can honestly say that I have never been short of money since that time.

On another occasion, whilst at Bible School my friend and I desperately wanted to go on a trip to the Holy Land organised by the church. We simply did not have the money, but we prayed about it and in faith put our names on the list to go. We arranged things so that everything would be covered while we were to be away and waited patiently for the cash to arrive. Finally, on the last Sunday by which payment had to be made, we had still seen no money forthcoming. However, having heard how God sometimes leaves things to the last minute, we did not cross out our names. We were just passing the church office when the Senior Pastor called us in, looking somewhat surprised, and announced the good news that someone had put up almost all the money for us to go on the trip. Nothing is over until it's over!

We should also realise that faith is not measured by quantity but quality. Jesus said, **'If you have faith as a mustard seed, you will say to this mountain, 'Move from here to there,' and it will move; and nothing will be impossible for you.'** Faith is watered and given life by the Word, **'For the Word of God is living and powerful.'** All we have to do is meditate on it.

We know that to meditate means to mutter, and it is a good idea to continually repeat God's promises to ourselves to maintain the strength of our faith. In his booklet, 'God's Creative Power', Charles Capps suggests bible verses that will help us by providing memory verses we can repeat throughout the day, especially concerning healing. As he says, Christianity is known as the Great Confession, but most Christians who are unsuccessful in obtaining God's promises are confessing the wrong things. It is a good idea to constantly remind ourselves of the promises of a loving and ever faithful God.

Charles Capps' recommendation to speak

God's Word (which he calls God's Medicine) over to ourselves several times a day, while awaiting the manifestation of our healing, is a great way to strengthen our faith.

Together with faith, James tells us that we must exercise patience. We have said that healing is not always miraculous and this is sometimes a test of our faith. Will it hold when we don't see immediate results? James 1:3 says, **'knowing that the testing of your faith produces patience.** [Verse 4] **But let patience have its perfect work.'** My impression has been that most people do not receive their healing because they give up too soon. God loves persistence and Jesus tells us to keep on asking God. Luke 11:8 says, **'I say to you that though he will not rise and give to him because he is his friend, yet because of his persistence he will rise and give him as many as he needs.'**

Hebrews 11:1 gives us the definition of faith: **'Now faith is the substance of things hoped for, the evidence of things not seen.'** It took me some time to unravel from this how faith actually works but it is explained if we read carefully. The 'substance or *hupostasis* (a setting under or support) is the framework of what we believe for, the confident assurance of what is to be which is not equally expressed by the word *elpis* or hope. The 'evidence' is the provision of proof of things not seen. How can we provide that? By behaving as if they were seen. If we can see them we don't need faith for them. By behaving as if God will do what He promised and providing the circumstances for it to happen, we then provide evidence of our faith.

The Gift of Faith (1 Corinthians 12:9) is a spiritual gift which usually accompanies gifts of healings or other special anointings, usually for a specific period. It seems to be a faith which comes upon us and empowers us to carry out specific tasks on perhaps one-off occasions. It does not seem to be a continuing faith covering everything.

There are specific laws which operate in the universe as a normal occurrence, such as the Law of Gravity. Paul tells us in Romans 3:27 that there is a Law of Faith, **'Where is boasting then? It is excluded. By what law? Of works? No, but**

by the law of faith.' Verse 28: **'Therefore we conclude that a man is justified by faith apart from the deeds of the law.'** The law of faith is operating in our lives all the time, whether we realise it or not. For example, every time we sit on a chair, we need faith that it will not collapse and send us to the floor. We need to make faith in the Word of God a more everyday habit.

There is also a spirit of faith. In 1 Corinthians 4:13 Paul says, **'And since we have the same spirit of faith, according to what is written...'** This is a spirit that is caught rather than taught. If we remember Caleb and the Promised Land, God says in Numbers 14:24, **'But my servant Caleb, because he has a different spirit in him and has followed me fully.'**

We need to develop a spirit of faith in what God says in order to bring about the promises of God. This is the way God has set things up. He cannot change His laws. We can either go along with them or miss out. Hebrews 2:4, Romans 1:17, Galatians 3:11 and Hebrews 10:38 all say **'The just shall live by faith'**. According to the law of faith, we must speak out what we want to see happen and disregard what we already see. People often approach God for healing with hit and miss attitude. Nothing will happen without faith on somebody's part. Genuine faith calls the power of the Holy Spirit to the scene and then things will happen. Faith is not believing that God will do it but that God has already done it.

Not taking God at His Word and having faith in Him to act is really a sin. In Hebrews 3:12 the writer says, **'Beware, brethren, lest there be in any of you an evil heart of unbelief in departing from the living God'**. If we believe we receive when we pray, then it is no longer valid for us to proclaim ourselves as sick. We are either sick or healed, one or the other, and we must decide for ourselves which it is. I am not suggesting this is an easy situation to cope with, but building a really strong faith on the Word will eventually get us there.

As well as positive faith for healing, we must not overlook the fact that faith can work in a negative way in the form of fear. Fear is destructive and dangerous and one of the devil's favourite weapons. But 2 Timothy 1:7 says, **'For God has not given us a spirit of fear but of power and of love and of a sound mind'**. If we keep in the Word and all the promises of God, we will destroy fear and prevent its destructive power in our lives.

We remember what harm fear did to Job. In chapter 3, verse 25, he says, **'For the thing I greatly feared has come upon me, And what I dreaded has happened to me.'** Fear is just as powerful at creating misfortune for us by allowing the devil to put on us what we believe will happen. We must say to ourselves, **'I am healed and whole in the name of Jesus Christ according to the truth of the Word.'**

It is quite usual for us all to be afraid at some time or other, but we have to remember that fear is the enemy of faith. We should try not to voice our fears because, as we have already seen, our words are constructive for bad things as well as good. If we are afraid we must a) keep it to ourselves b) go back to the Bible and read about the total goodness of God which should dispel all our fears

We must visualise ourselves as healed and whole and hold on to that thought through thick and thin. We must not let the devil put ungodly thoughts into our heads. It can be extremely difficult to disregard a doctor's report and hang on to God's Word when we don't see any change. Especially when we may feel guilt about consulting a doctor because of our lack of faith in God. Will God forgive me for going to a doctor? Of course He will if our faith in Him is not yet strong enough, but it is not His best for us. He is a loving and all-forgiving God and we have no need to feel guilt about anything. This will not help the situation.

The one drawback is the fact that doctors' medications often have side effects which can then appear as part of the sickness. This can confuse the issue. It may not bring God glory that we go to the doctor, but why would he be against them when they help so many people? I can only repeat that it is not God's best for us. After all, He made us and best knows how to heal us. And needless to say, with God there are no side effects!

Chapter 7

HOW DOES GOD'S HEALING POWER WORK?

It would be very arrogant and stupid to say we know exactly how God's power works. It is limitless, unimaginably varied and stupendously effective. There are, however, characteristics that we can observe and information contained in the Word of God that help us to understand a little about it.

Firstly, what is it like? It is almost universally

agreed that it exists in a form something like electricity, which, on occasion, can be felt. After all, we cannot see mobile phone waves but we know they exist. I have not come across any claim that they are tangible.

Certainly, God's healing power is tangible on occasion. We are told in the Bible that when the woman with the issue of blood touched Jesus' clothing, power went out of him to heal her. Mark 5:30 says, **'And Jesus, immediately knowing in Himself that power had gone out of Him, turned around to the crowd and said, 'Who touched me?'**

Another characteristic would be that this power is unlimited. Luke 6:17 tells us, **'And He came down with them and stood on a level place with a crowd of His disciples and a great multitude of people from all Judea and Jerusalem, and from the seacoast of Tyre and Sidon; who came to hear Him and be healed of their diseases** [Verse 18], **as well as those who were tormented with unclean spirits, And they were healed** [Verse 19], **and**

the whole multitude sought to touch Him, for power went out from Him and healed them all.'

This tangibility transferred through the clothing is evident again in Acts 12:11, 12 where we are told: **'Now God worked unusual miracles by the hands of Paul, so that even handkerchiefs or aprons were brought from his body to the sick and the diseases left them and the evil spirits went out of them.'** This method of healing is still used today when Christians pray over prayer cloths which are later brought into contact with sick people (sometimes hidden under the pillow) to bring about their healing.

A more usual method of healing today is through the laying on of hands, as instructed by Jesus in Mark 16:15. It is not uncommon for the healing power to be felt to move from one person to another, although the fact that there is no tangible sense of power does not mean that it is absent. Indeed, it has been further suggested that the power may enter a person and remain dormant there until activated. This is described in his excellent book 'Getting Healed' by Derek Walker.

We could imagine healing power as contained in a torch battery. The power is present, the bulb is in place but there will be no light until the power is activated by the switch. In the incident involving the paralysed man in Luke 5, many people were present to hear Jesus. We are told, **'And the power of the Lord was present to heal them'.** Only one man was healed on that occasion, a man whose friends had enough faith to lower him through the roof because they were confident that Jesus would heal him.

Kenneth E Hagin says in his book *Seven Things You Should Know About Divine Healing* that the healing power of God is a tangible force, and describes the laying on of hands as calling into being 'The Law of Contact and Transmission'. He mentions God's healing anointing such as that possessed by Jesus, but says that faith must be present in the recipient. It appears that faith acts as the switch which connects God's healing power to the recipient. This switch, however, is not a one-off action; it must be kept on, otherwise the healing can be lost.

It has been suggested that the person can be healed through the faith of the person ministering healing. This would account for the many who believe they receive their healing at a meeting or crusade, only to find later that they have lost their healing because they personally do not have faith to maintain it. This is why it is important that faith is real heart knowledge, derived from the Word. This kind of faith cannot be lost.

John G Lake, the great instigator of the famous Healing Rooms in Spokane, Washington, where 100,000 people were certified as healed in five years, was a medical student in his early years. He became interested in measuring healing activity in connection with the Word with specially-designed equipment. He leads us to believe that the cortex of the brain is affected when, through reciting the Word of God, the Spirit of God comes upon us and comes into the soul, taking possession of the brain. Then the whole body becomes alive with the life of God and the nature of God and healing takes place. His comment on one healing was, 'All there is to it is that the life of God comes back into the part that is afflicted, and right away the blood flows in and the work is done.'

One thing we can be sure of is that God wants us healed, because He has provided all we need for our healing. It is up to us to claim in faith, nothing wavering, what is ours by right.

Chapter 8

WHAT'S THIS BELIEVER'S AUTHORITY I HEARD ABOUT?

Authority is delegated power. Our authority over sickness comes to us from Jesus, who conquered sin and sickness when he died on the cross. A policeman in uniform has the power to step out into the road and hold up his hand and immediately the traffic will come to a halt. This is because he has the authority delegated to him by the local authority to do just that. If you or I stepped out into the road and held up our hands to stop the traffic, I doubt the result would be the same.

On several occasions Jesus sent out His disciples with His delegated authority to heal and deliver people. Luke 10:19: **'Behold, I give you authority** [Strongs 1849 exousia - authority to exercise power] **to trample on serpents and scorpions, and over all the power** [Strongs 1411 dunamis - practical, active power] **of the enemy, and nothing shall by any means hurt you'.** We receive the same authority when we are born again because of the New Covenant made for us through Jesus' death on the cross.

If we recollect, a covenant involved an exchange of power, authority and responsibility and we inherited all these at the new birth. 2 Corinthians 5:17 says, **'Therefore if anyone is in Christ, he is a new creation; old things have passed away; behold all things have become new'.** Jesus gave us His robe of righteousness for our old sin covering and we now have power over disease and evil spirits just as

Jesus has. This is very hard for some of us to grasp. To have such power is, admittedly, mind-blowing and difficult to absorb immediately. In other words, it takes time to get used to this new status and many Christians, although born again, remain ignorant of their rights as sons and daughters of God. Here again, we can quote Hosea 4:6: **'My people are destroyed for lack of knowledge'.**

There is the story of the man found dead in a small, shabby room which he rented for £3 per week. He had been a familiar sight for almost 20 years, dressed in rags and eating out of garbage cans. When he was not seen for two or three days, concerned neighbours looked for him. As he was found dead in bed, there was an autopsy which confirmed that he had died from malnutrition. Yet he was wearing around his waist a money belt with over £23,000 in it. His life could have been so different if only he had used that which had belonged to him all along.

Because Jesus has made us righteous, the devil no longer has any authority in our lives. He can only do us harm if we allow him to. Job allowed him to put fear on him and gave the devil access. He will put fear on us if we let him. But 2 Timothy 1:7 says, **'For God has not given us a spirit of fear, but of power and of love, and of a sound mind.'** If we constantly fear what the devil can do to us, we are giving him access to our lives that he has no right to and the authority to harm us, instead of using our delegated power to oust him. James 4:7 says, **'Resist the devil and he will flee from you'.** We are to submit to God, not the devil.

How does this robe of righteousness work? Under the Old Covenant we would be responsible for our sins of disobedience, which were expiated or covered each year by the priest in the temple. Jesus performed a once-for-all expiation, reconciling us to God, so that provided we repent our sins are no longer held against us and we are no longer fair game for the devil. We are now covered by the blood of Jesus. This does not mean that Satan will leave us alone, but we have the legal right to send him packing.

Healing is a legally accomplished work on our behalf. When Jesus said on the cross, at the very last, the word 'tetelestai', He made that very point. The word is a market place term meaning 'account paid in full - nothing owing'. All our sins were paid for when He went down into Hell to complete Satan's defeat. **'Having disarmed principalities and powers, He made a public spectacle of them, triumphing over them in it'** (Colossians 2:15). The devil can put symptoms on us but he cannot make us accept them if we refuse. We simply have to tell him to go. Our complete healing has been bought and paid for by Jesus and we are technically healed and whole, 'nothing missing, nothing broken', as Gloria Copeland puts it. In reality, we are not sick people trying to get healed, we are healed and whole people whom the devil is trying to keep sick.

We do not have to accept sickness because it is not legally ours if we are born again. The devil is a defeated foe, his days are numbered and he knows it. He is simply trying to destroy as many of God's people as he can in the short time left to him. We must remember that we are in a covenant relationship with God, so there is no question of our authority not being made good.

Matthew 28:18 says, **'And Jesus came to them and said 'All authority in heaven and earth has been given to me'.** When He ascended into heaven, He transferred His authority to His church. He is the head of the church and we are the body i.e. we are Christ's hands and feet here on earth. In Mark 15, **'He said to them 'Go into all the world and preach the gospel to every creature... And these signs will follow those who believe In My name they will cast out demons, they will speak with new tongues; they will take up serpents and if they drink any deadly thing it will by no means hurt them; they will lay hands on the sick and they will recover'.**

Christians are not sure of their authority over disease because it seems that it is largely not taught in churches today. It is easy to see that one of the reasons for this is to avoid disappointment when healing is not manifested on any one occasion. And yet the Bible tells us very plainly that Jesus gave us His authority. John 14:13 says that Jesus said, **'And whatever you ask in my Name, that will I do, that the Father may be glorified in the Son. If you ask** [demand] **anything in my name, I will do it.'** When I was at Bible School, I was blessed with an instructor who asked us every day, 'Do you know who you are in Jesus?' It may take a while to sink in but when we act in faith in the Name of Jesus, believing we have His full authority, the devil has to concede to us in whatever we are claiming.

Ephesians 2:4 says, **'But God, who is rich in mercy, because of His great love with which He loved us, even when we were dead in trespasses, made us alive together with Christ... and raised us up together, and made us to sit together in the heavenly places in Christ Jesus,'**. We are joint heirs with Him, being **'predestined to adoption as sons'** (Ephesians 1:5). Verse 21 says that Jesus has been set, **'Far above all principality and power *(exousia)* and might and dominion**

and every name that is named, not only in this age but in that which is to come.'

The source of our authority is found in the resurrection and exalting of Christ by God. When we realise that the authority that belongs to Christ also belongs to the individual members of the body of Christ AND IS AVAILABLE TO US, our lives will be revolutionised. It is a question of bringing Kingdom of God principles to Earth, so that God's will is done here on Earth as it is in Heaven (Lord's Prayer).

Matthew 10:7 says, **'And as you go, preach, saying, the kingdom of heaven is at hand, heal the sick.'** Matthew 16:19 says, **'I will give you the keys to the kingdom of heaven.'** Matthew 18:18 says, **'Assuredly, I say to you, whatever you bind on earth will be bound in heaven, and whatever you loose on earth will be loosed in heaven.'** When Jesus began to preach, in Mark 4:17 He told them to **'repent for the kingdom of heaven was at hand.'** Where we are, kingdom principles must apply.

John Alexander Dowie, a Scotsman who

received a revelation about divine healing while ministering before the turn of the century in Australia, crossed the ocean many times. He encountered many storms, but every time one appeared he did what Jesus did. He rebuked the storm and it ceased. He knew he had the authority to do this.

When He worked on earth, Jesus operated in His anointing as a man, and not as God (Philippians 2:7). Things were different, however, after He had died and completely defeated the devil. In John 14:12, Jesus says, **'Most assuredly, I say to you, he who believes in Me, the works that I do will he do also; and greater works than these will he do, because I go to My Father.'**

Many problems exist because we allow them to. We often try to get someone else to do something, including God. In many instances, such as healing, God has already done it all. He has given us the victory through Jesus Christ and He has given us the authority to enforce that victory. We simply need to put Him in remembrance of His Word. We are already blessed, healed, forgiven, saved, redeemed, delivered, accepted, set free and reigning in this life. It is up to us to appropriate these victories and not to allow the devil to steal them from us.

Whilst we should rejoice in the power and authority given to us by Jesus, we should also recognise its limitations. We have authority over the devil in our own lives and families, but we have no right to try to exercise authority over someone else or their household without their permission. When we pray with people who are sick, they need to humble themselves before God and give us permission to speak into their lives. God will never go against a person's will, and nor must we.

We should never pray for people in a church without the permission of the pastor who is the spiritual head of the church, just as the husband is the spiritual head of the family. Jesus always respected authority: **'Render unto Caesar that which is Caesar's'** (Matthew 22:21). God expects us to keep the law and respect authority unless it goes against His will. We must always respect other people's authority if we expect the devil to recognise ours.

The exercise of authority is clearly dealt with in Jesus' meeting with the centurion (Matthew 8:8). Not only did the man recognise Jesus' supreme authority over sickness, he understood that distance was no barrier to the effectiveness of Jesus' healing power.

We have God-given authority over every sickness that exists in the world today, if only we can have the faith to use it.

Chapter 9

WHAT CAN WE LEARN FROM THE MINISTRY OF JESUS?

It seems that Jesus did nothing significant in His life concerning His ministry until He received the Baptism of the Holy Spirit from His cousin John (John 1:32). Even after this, at the wedding at Cana in Galilee, He told His mother when she asked for a miracle, **'My hour is not yet come'** (John 2:4).

He did finally announce His ministry in Luke 4:15 when He stood up in the synagogue and read from the prophet Isaiah and made several important points. Firstly, He told them that He had been baptised in the Spirit and that He was anointed to do what He had come to do, which was to preach, to heal, to proclaim recovery and sight and, most importantly, to proclaim 'the acceptable year of the Lord'. This statement would have been of great significance to the Jews because the acceptable year only came round every 50 years. This was the time when land was returned to its original owners and slaves were set free – a recognised time of restoration.

At first, they **'marvelled at the gracious words which proceeded out of His mouth'** but it was not long before they were **'filled with wrath and rose up and thrust Him out of the city and led Him to a brow of the hill on which their city was built, that they might throw Him down over the cliff'** (verse29). After which Jesus began His ministry in Capernaum, starting by dealing with several unclean spirits.

The method of healing most connected with Him, however, is the laying on of hands, and this is the method most in use today, although it is by no means the only way God heals people today. The reason this method is so popular seems to be the Transmission of Power described in an earlier chapter. Sometimes the power of God can be felt to travel through the person ministering into the person receiving healing but this is not always the case.

There is a great need for the person receiving ministry to be receptive of their healing. Although power is present, unless it is received in faith, it can be rendered dormant and ineffective in that instance. Where there is a strong healing anointing present, as there certainly was with Jesus, the presence of the Holy Spirit is not questioned, but when laying hands on the sick today it is always wise to invoke the presence of the Holy Spirit. It is also imperative to do as Jesus commanded in Mark 11:23 and command the 'mountain' of sickness to leave. Whilst any experience of power is not significant to the healing it sometimes happens that the person can fall down under the power and it is best to be prepared for this. Also, whilst it is quite normal for the eyes to be closed while praying, this is not a good idea for the person ministering who needs to be alert to any reaction in the person being prayed with.

We should also remember that Jesus and His disciples used healing to 'confirm the Word with signs following'. If the Word of God is not spoken when we pray for people we are surely limiting what God can do, if we don't give Him anything to confirm.

When Jesus sent out His disciples to heal the sick, it is probable that they used His method of the laying on of hands. However, this was not always possible and not always Jesus' choice. The woman with the issue of blood, for example, touched Him (Mark 5:27) to receive her healing power. In the case of blind Bartimaeus, who had illustrated his faith by throwing aside his coat, which it is suggested was a badge of his disability by virtue of its colour, there is no mention of Jesus having touched him (Mark 11:52). In Luke 7, when Jesus heard about the centurion's servant, before He had even reached the house, the servant was reported as being no longer sick. So it seems that while the laying on of hands is the most popular method of ministering healing, it is not vital to the healing process and certainly not where faith has already been demonstrated. Jesus always asked questions which brought people to a position where they could release their faith, thereby releasing an expectation of healing.

There have been many cases of healing at a distance and people can certainly receive healing over the telephone when faith becomes operative. If we agree with the suggestion that whatever is felt, power is implanted through the laying on of hands, power which may be stored to remain dormant for a while, as suggested by Derek Walker in his book *Getting Healed*, it is likely to remain the most popular method of ministering healing.

Jesus almost always mentions faith at the scene of a healing and it is certain that faith must be present somewhere to activate the power. Whether the faith of the person ministering plays a part in this cannot be proved, except for the fact that some people who are apparently healed do seem to lose their healing at a later date. This is catalogued in reports of the many healing crusades of the early nineteenth century. We can only assume that after healing, faith in the healer must be maintained and it is the responsibility of the healed person to see that it is.

When there is a special healing meeting and an obvious anointing on the person ministering, giving rise to a great feeling of expectancy among the participants, it is not unusual for several people at once to receive healing without being touched at all. It is likely that this happened in Jesus' time because of the volume of people healed on occasion but it is not expressly reported and He may have laid hands on the whole crowd individually.

Some things we do know about Jesus' ministry:

He never turned anyone away.

He was never too busy.

He had no favourites.

He never said it was not the right time for

someone to be healed.

He never said the healing was too difficult.

'And Jesus Christ is the same, yesterday, today and forever' (Hebrews 13:8)

Chapter 10

I'VE DONE ALL THAT AND I'M STILL NOT HEALED

This is the point at which many people become frustrated and begin looking for someone or something to blame. Expressions such as 'God doesn't heal everyone' and 'the person who prayed for me wasn't anointed' come to mind.

Because the devil likes to destroy God's work in any way he can, it follows that he will put as many obstacles between us and our healing as we either consciously or unconsciously allow. Some are more obvious than others, and some we can be totally unaware of, but we have the Holy Spirit, the Comforter, to help us in this. Just because we haven't yet seen the desired result does not mean our healing is permanently out of reach and we must continue to press in for the answer. There may be some small thing that we have overlooked which is causing the problem. For instance, we know that unforgiveness towards others is a biggie, especially when we don't realise we are holding on to it, but how many of us realise that we must also forgive ourselves. This is just as important to God, who has forgiven us everything through His Son.

Doubt and unbelief play a major part in preventing healing. We recall that Jesus could not perform the healings that He wished to in his home town of Nazareth because of their unbelief (Matthew 13:58). Even the disciples were guilty of unbelief on occasion. In Matthew 17:19 they asked, **'Why could we not cast it out?'** In verse 20, Jesus replies, **'Because of your unbelief.'**

There are instances in the ministry of Jesus that are used to encourage doubts about healing. Why did only one man get healed at the Pool of Bethesda (John 5:2) and why did the blind man, who at first only saw **'men as trees walking'** (Mark 8:24), have to be prayed for a second time? No answers are obvious except that Jesus had not finally defeated the devil by His death on the cross and was as prone to obstacles as we can be. However, we have no excuse, as Jesus soundly defeated every aspect of the devil's power in John 14:12: **'Greater things than this will ye do.'**

Doubt and unbelief do not exist without a reason and we can overcome them by identifying the reasons and dealing with them systematically. The blatant remark that we don't have enough faith is wrong because we have noticed that it is quality of faith that matters. What happens is that we allow our faith to be overshadowed by doubts which allow reasons for not getting healed to become more acceptable to us than the Word of God.

Dr. Roger Sapp has written an excellent book

which deals with personal doubts entitled, *Without a Shadow of a Doubt*. In this he analyses these individual doubts and suggests how to deal with them. God's willingness to heal and timing are brought into question. Are we being presumptive in requesting healing – after all our friend didn't get healed? Any experiences we have had in the past can come into play to strengthen our reasons to doubt our eligibility for healing, and most of them are contrary to the Word of God, as we have already seen.

Most doubts spring from an incomplete understanding and acceptance of the Word but sometimes a prophecy from the past holding a promise of healing on a certain occasion can cloud the issue and misdirect faith. I once met a person holding on to a 31-year-old prophecy concerning her healing which she was still waiting for. It should be noted that all such prophecy should be confirmed by a separate source and not accepted willy nilly. Whatever the cause of doubt, it will be very real to the person concerned and should be dealt with as gently as possible. We should also confirm with the person that it is a genuine doubt, and not a reluctance on their part to cope with the very real changes in circumstances and perhaps relationships that their healing might bring. Some people just don't want to be healed but may not want to admit it. They may already know what the obstacle to their healing is, but don't want to change. If there is a genuine desire for healing, then we must continue to seek to identify the obstacle.

It is also wise to check what activities we are engaged in and what their spiritual significance might be. It often surprises people to know that yoga, Pilates and any exercise based on an ancient religion can harbour unwanted spiritual forces. Fortune-telling, ouija boards and ESP are all alien to Christianity and offensive to God. It is worth checking that we are not harbouring in our homes anything with unscriptural connotations such as books, statuettes and objects from religions other than Christianity. Some statuettes have hiding places specially prepared to house the spirit of that religion and by holding on to these objects we can unknowingly open the door to evil spirits.

When we look at the concept of God described in the Ten Commandments and how He regards other gods, we are told that He is a jealous God. Most people would not want to take chances and my advice to them would be, 'If in doubt, throw it out!' Those who consider that in the light of the New Covenant, the Old Testament Commandments have no relevance today should examine the evidence of those who have dabbled in witchcraft, failed to honour their parents and not taken a rest day as they should. Many accounts exist of people who have recovered their health when these sins have been put right and repented of. Freemasonry is an activity which many people regard as a Godly brotherhood, not realising the danger of its connection with the devil.

Besides the existence of objects bringing curses in the form of demonic influence upon people, word curses and self-curses are just as powerful. Once again I would stress that there is nothing to fear because there is nothing that cannot be put right with God. We can firstly curse ourselves by speaking things about us and our future which, if said with enough faith, will undoubtedly come to pass. 'I think I'm getting a cold', or 'I'm so tired' are popular sayings. When we know the obedience of our bodies to what we say, we realise that our bodies will immediately go into the right mode to bring about what we have said, and demons are all too ready to assist.

As well as cursing ourselves, other people can put word curses on us if we take on board what they say. Anything we receive as true which does not line up with the word of God can let the devil in. Teachers and parents have a great responsibility for what they speak over a child. Children can be badly affected by such statements as, 'You'll never be any good at that' or 'You'll never amount to much'. It is not easy, if we are sensitive beings, to avoid taking these things on board but we must hold on to God's view of us. He loves us to bits and thinks we are 'the bees knees'. Certainly we make mistakes and don't come up to expectations, but as long as we truly repent we are forgiven. **'As far as the East is from the West, So far has He removed our transgressions from us'** (Psalm 103:12). Seeds are planted in us through what people say about us, but they will only grow if we allow them to.

Promiscuity and sex outside marriage can have a far more damaging effect on us than we realise. We may say that we have repented of that and believe that it is over and done with, and this may be true. However, we know that the Bible says that when two people marry they become one person. This means that a spiritual bond is formed and evil spirits can easily be passed from one to the other. These happenings are known as 'ungodly soul ties' and need to be dealt with on a deliverance basis.

So we see there are many avenues that the devil will use to spoil our relationship with God and thereby rob us of our healing. It is not always easy to put a finger on the sin causing the obstacle. But as in all things, persistence pays, because we know that God likes persistence (Luke 11:8: **'yet because of his persistence he will**

rise and give him as many as he needs.' If we need to deal with the demonic in order to receive the manifestation of our healing, we must go after it. There is help available.

We know that sin gives the devil authority in our lives to bring misfortune, including sickness. We have seen that there is no good reason for sickness to exist on its own. Whatever the situation, it need only be temporary if we are willing to do something about it and a dedicated search may be called for.

Gordon Cove, a healing evangelist in the early 1900s, wrote a book on the barriers to healing he discovered during his crusades. He lists 40 of the more general ones. It is amazing how we can be harbouring unforgiveness, anger, murmuring and other disqualifiers without realising it. We have already dealt with the sins of the tongue. The first he lists are that people are prayed for prematurely, before adequate preparation, and this is probably the biggest obstacle. The Word on healing is not generally taught in churches today, so that there is no widespread knowledge of how it works according to the Word.

Because of lack of teaching, Jesus is not so much regarded as a healer today as He was in the early days of the church. This also ties in with the fact that some people who are told they are born again do not have a full understanding of the concept and the real need for repentance that is required for this to benefit them. A single prayer of dedication of our lives to Jesus does not qualify us without full repentance and possible changes in our lives. These people are not to blame for situations where they may be left with demonic influences in their lives.

It seems that in the early days of Christianity people were released from evil spirits before they were baptised. (Perhaps one example of this is when Philip visited Samaria, in Acts Chapter 8.) With the seeming reluctance of churches today to tackle demonic issues, this process is not often carried out. Because we have Jesus' authority, I repeat once again that evil spirits need never be feared and can easily be dealt with. Because of our natural fear of spiritual things and the tendency for most churches to sweep them under the carpet, many Christians wrestle with bad spiritual influences. Besides fear of the unknown, it may be that a church leader may fear the loss of many of his congregation if he were to delve too deeply into spiritual matters.

So apart from specialist deliverance ministries, demonic beings are largely left alone to do their work unhindered. Since it has been suggested by leading ministries that demonic forces are responsible for 70%-80% of all sickness, it is hardly surprising that there is so much sickness in the Christian church today. Whilst the fear of demons in understandable, we cannot ignore Jesus instructions to deal with them (Mark 6:7 and 16:17) for which He has given us His fullest authority.

The best illustration I have been given of lurking demonic influences is to imagine I have purchased a house freehold and gone along to examine my purchase, believing it to be vacant. On arrival, I find a family living upstairs who show me a document, agreed to by the previous owner, stating that they had a perfectly legal right to be there. To get them out I will have to go to court. In many cases, born-again Christians need to take the devil to court for Jesus to gain full possession of their property.

If there is an obstacle to our healing, it is not in God's interests to withhold that information from us, and we should search diligently for the answer.

John G Lake is recorded as saying, 'God's chariot will come down the road when all the stones are out of the way,' and he showed by his results that he knew what he was talking about!

Chapter 11

WHAT ABOUT THE DEMONS JESUS MENTIONED?

We note from Luke 4:33 that the first healing carried out by Jesus was delivering a man of evil spirits. This is also the first thing He mentions in His instructions to the disciples concerning the power of believers to carry out things in His name. It was obviously an important part of His ministry and therefore should be an important part of ours.

The chief thing to remember about demons or evil spirits is that they can only remain and do mischief where they have a legal right to be, i.e. if we do nothing about them. What we have to do is exactly what Jesus did, and that is to cast them out. To do this, we need to fully understand the believer's authority given to us by Jesus. Demons recognise this authority and have to leave when they are told, forbidden to return.

Why are demons present in the first place? To deal with them effectively we must first attempt to discover why they are present, and this is not always easy. However, some demons are quite self-assured and will announce their right to remain to you, using the voice of the person concerned.

What would make us suspect the presence of a demonic influence? Things like an addictive habit, an urge to get into sin that the believer knows is entirely wrong, or a recurring temptation of any sort or a sickness that will not go away and has maybe come down the family line. An attraction to pornography etc. or the sense of an evil presence. There is sometimes a generational predisposition to an addiction which is inherited when familiar spirits have come down through the family line. Where there is no knowledge or acceptance of a generational trait, it is always safest to assume that there is a demonic influence at work and deal with it accordingly.

If we are unsure what the problem is, it is best to cover all possibilities, and this can be done through comprehensive repentance and prayer. In his excellent book *They Shall Expel Demons* Derek Prince provides a complete prayer, a 'Prayer To Be Set Free', which should cover most eventualities in expelling demons. Then it is straight into the Word of God to keep them out. If we speak in tongues, this is a good defence as demons are scared because they can't understand it.

A group of dedicated Christians praying together are well able to deal with the demonic if they are assured of their authority through Jesus Christ. However, spirits can easily return unless the door is closed on them by removing their legal right to be present. It seems that the early church knew far more about dealing with the demonic than we do today, probably because the need for genuine repentance seems to have been stressed more that it is in today's churches. The power of sin is largely in its secrecy and once it is in the open its power is partly destroyed. James 5:16 encourages us to **'Confess your trespasses to one another, and pray for one another, that you may be healed'**.

Possibly one of the fears today is that the situation may be made worse, perhaps because of Jesus' comments in Matthew 12:43-45: **'When an unclean spirit goes out of a man, he goes through dry places, seeking rest, and finds none. Then he says, 'I will return to my house from which I came.' And when he comes, he finds it empty, swept, and put in order. Then he goes and takes with him seven other spirits more wicked than himself, and they enter and dwell there; and the last state of that man is worse than the first. So shall it also be with this wicked generation.'** This indicates that we should ensure that we are filled with the Holy Spirit and continually renew our minds to the Word of God to prevent us from falling back into old, familiar sins. The devil is very vigilant and will not miss any opportunity we give him.

Whilst some churches pay lip service to healing ministry with spasmodic sessions of the laying on of hands, it would be fair to say that most churches have no idea what to do about evil spirits or demons. On the occasions when unfortunate individuals have been the victims of manifestations of evil spirits, those church members who have not panicked have done very little to remedy the situation. People seem to hastily pray in tongues or stare in disbelief until the spirit tires of the exhibition.

There is a lamentable lack of enthusiasm in dealing with this sort of phenomenon and incidents are swiftly swept under the carpet with no real result or concern for the person involved. When we realise from information from Deliverance Ministries that at least 70-80% of all sickness and disease is caused directly or indirectly by demonic forces, this seems feeble, to say the least. There is, of course, an unwillingness to own up to this in case serious action is called for. When we hear a pastor teach that a Christian can't have a demon (oh that this were so), we realise that the overall situation is largely a problem of wrong teaching in the church. Certainly, a Christian cannot be possessed by a demon, having given their life to Jesus, but they can certainly be attacked by them. Not only can they be seen, by certain gifted people, to be attached to people, but their activity can be seen as they exit through the fingers or are expelled through the mouth.

I would stress once again that demons are not to be feared. They are, on the whole, pathetic creatures who are capable of such remarks as, 'You can't get rid of me, I'm not here'. Insistence that they depart in the Name of Jesus Christ of Nazareth is usually all that is required - that is unless the person concerned wants to keep them. It does happen!

Their main fear seems to be that they will lose their 'house' and become homeless. In Mark 5:12, after they begged him, Jesus gave them permission to enter the swine. In the same way that they recognised His authority, they must recognise the delegated authority of a believer who knows who they are in Jesus. In Mark 15:16 we see that Jesus expressly gave all believers the authority to cast out demons.

Where do demons come from? We have already discussed the possibility of their having been inherited from the activities of a previous generation, sins that we cannot possibly know anything about. In Daniel 9:5 we read that Daniel is praying earnestly to God and confessing the sins of his ancestors at some length. We note in Nehemiah 1:6 that Nehemiah is doing exactly the same thing.

It is generally accepted that the 'familiar' spirits spoken of in the Old Testament are inherited demons, probably from generational sin. Unfortunately, ignorance does not absolve us from the responsibility of removing them from our lives. The good news is that as soon as we can put our finger on what is allowing them to stay, they have to leave. We can get help with this from the

Holy Spirit and praying friends. With the personal sin of unforgiveness the most common and other sins that we may be conscious of, or sin brought to light by the Holy Spirit, demons will leave when the sin is repented of because it no longer has a hold on us.

It can be a little more difficult when sin is of a generational origin, which for the most part we would be unaware of. Most churches have no idea what to do in these cases but, for the persistent, there is plenty of help at hand if we know where to look. Sin is usually the cause, because nowhere in the Bible does God Commit Himself to forgive sins that have not been repented of (Derek Prince). Here I must mention again that being born again does not automatically deal with our past sin or generational sin. Only a total repentance of our own sins and those of our ancestors, and a total acceptance of what Jesus did on the cross, can wipe the slate clean and free us from the persistence of demons. The Bible says that **'God has not given us a spirit of fear but of power and of love and of a sound mind'** (2 Timothy

1:7) and we are to use this power against demonic forces.

As I have said, most churches tend to ignore the presence of the demonic and many, many people are sick unnecessarily because they have not been taught what Jesus intended us to know. The devil is having a field day in churches where the people refuse to wake up to the truth of scripture. Paul warns us in Ephesians 6:12 that **'we do not wrestle against flesh and blood, but against principalities, against powers, against the rulers of the darkness of this age, against spiritual hosts of wickedness in the heavenly places'.**

So where do we get help, if not from the church? I have already mentioned that there are many ministries and books that deal with all aspects of healing and demonic forces. Ellel Grange is is an International Ministry based in Lancaster with at least three centres in this country where people can learn about the demonic. Bill Subritzky, who died recently aged 90, had a wonderful ministry in New Zealand. He had the advantage of being able to see demons. Derek Prince Ministries have both books and DVDs on the subject and there are many others.

Perhaps it should be mentioned here that any deliverance ministry that does take place in a church must be with the permission and under the spiritual covering of the pastor. We know that God likes things done in order and under proper authority. Only if we respect authority will the devil respect ours.

Chapter 12

WHAT NOW?

If we have received a manifestation of our healing, we should remember to give God all the glory and tell everyone we meet. We should encourage others to seek their healing.

If we have not yet arrived at the place where our 'faith as a mustard seed' has produced the required manifestation, we should not give up. Hebrews 6:12 tells us that faith and patience work together to inherit the promises of God. James **1:17 says, 'Every good gift and every perfect**

gift is from above, and comes down from the Father of lights, with whom there is no variation or shadow of turning.' Sometimes our faith needs to be confirmed by constant reference to the Word.

In Andrew Wommack's teaching on what to do when it doesn't look like you're healed in his CD series 'God Wants You Well', he suggests that God gives us the answer to prayer immediately but that through incorrect teaching we are not always able to receive it immediately. He says that faith is based on knowledge and therefore incorrect knowledge leads to incorrect faith. He says that faith is the substance that gives physical appearance to the healing that God has already provided in the spirit world. Because God is a spiritual, not a physical being, our prayers are answered spiritually and the physical manifestation is brought about by the maintenance of our faith. This confirms the belief that what we say or think immediately after praying can influence the speed at which we receive our healing.

I cannot recommend too highly Derek Walker's book *Getting Healed*, which has already been mentioned. It contains all the Bible references we need to get the job done, and if we are relying on the Word of God alone, which is perfectly adequate, this is the book containing help of the first order. His church in Oxfordshire also has a healing team and holds services where prayer is available. Kenneth Copeland Ministries (KCM) is contactable online with information and encouragement.

If we attend churches where the leader is not well disposed towards healing ministry, we should not be discouraged. We can always find church members who have attended charismatic or Pentecostal churches who will understand your need (there are always one or two lurking in the background). If the leader is put off by James 5:14, **'Is anyone among you sick? Let him call for the elders of the church, and let them pray over him, anointing him with oil in the name of the Lord'**, it should be pointed out that the first word used for 'sick' is 'a*stheneo*', (Strongs 770), meaning 'weak, feeble, impotent (having no strength), and the second word used for sick is '*kamno*' (Strongs 2577), meaning to be weary from the effect of constant work. Vines describes them as being 'weary' and 'burnt out'. Neither term is the one normally used for sickness, which is '*nosos*' (Strongs 3554). Members of the Jerusalem church were allowed to become worn out, but not sick!

Unfortunately, from this chapter many people have assumed that only elders and pastors may pray for the sick and this has greatly limited the scope of believers who know the authority given by Jesus and His instructions in Mark 16:15. F F Bosworth in his book *Christ the Healer* quotes Dr R A Torrey in his book *Divine Healing* as saying: 'Individual believers, whether Elders or not, have the privilege and duty to pray for one another in case of sickness, with the expectation that God will hear and heal.' Whatever the situation, we should never pray for the sick at any church without the full consent of the church leader. The leader's authority must never be undermined.

Authority over sickness belongs to those who

believe that Jesus dealt with all our sickness on the cross so that we would be given authority in His name over all sickness and the works of Satan, having been set free from the lasting effects of sin. To pray for the sick without this confidence in the Atonement must be a very hit and miss affair. People who do this are firstly praying for something that they cannot be sure they have a right to, and secondly they have no guarantee that God hears their prayer (anything according to His will) or will do it anyway. Their excuse for failures is that God doesn't heal everyone, but no explanation has been forthcoming about how God chooses whom He will heal. Nor can they explain how being sick makes them a better person, which many claim. Certainly, if we are unsure of the truth of the Bible we really have no foundation for praying with someone for their healing to manifest. Because He is such a loving God, full of goodness and grace, some do get healed anyway, in spite of our lack of understanding.

When people go forward to receive healing

where no mention of God's healing power or the work of Jesus is made, there is no reminder of God's will to see His people well and of His great love, and therefore nothing on which to base an expectation for healing. To call for a healing line after preaching on a totally different subject is to lessen the possibility of success amongst the applicants. No expectation is created and many go forward with a halfhearted hope that something may happen. It seems that if only half the gospel is preached, only half the benefits will be received, which is in keeping with how God works.

Even when praying on the streets with people, speaking about God's love for us and the power of the Holy Spirit will bring healing power on the scene to bring about whatever is required. Dr John G Lake said, 'If we could make the world understand the pregnant vitality of the Spirit of God, man would discover that healing is not only a matter of faith, and a matter of the Grace of God, but a perfectly scientific application of God's Spirit to man's needs'. People have been healed on the streets who barely knew the name of Jesus when healing prayer has been made in the right context, i.e. accompanied by the Word and the people have been receptive to a healing God.

Does going to a medical doctor disqualify us from receiving healing from God? Of course not. Nothing disqualifies anyone from turning to Jesus. It goes without saying, however, that no one can fully have two beliefs at once and we must really decide where our faith lies. When we ask to be prayed for, we must leave in faith, believing that God is as good as His Word. We must also be aware that when we receive the manifestation of our healing, the first thing the devil will do is to try to steal it from us. But if our faith has been adequately maintained, it is impossible for the healing to be lost.

It is generally advised to always pray with a group of two or more people, preferably mixed, never with one person alone, and get them to lay hands on you if they are believers. If you have people who pray in tongues, it makes the devil nervous because he can't understand them. Call on the presence and power of the Holy Spirit.

Remind God that He is your healer and has promised healing through Jesus Christ. Speak to the problem or disease and command it to go. Receive your healing and thank God for it. Speak nothing negative about your situation and give all the glory to God.

Other places besides churches where prayer can be received include street ministries, which mostly have special regular days in the month when they send out a specially-trained team to pray with those in need. The City of Bath has such a team (HOTS - Healing On The Streets) and they are usually set up outside the Abbey for several days a week during the more clement months. Gloucester City also has a team for street ministry, as I am sure do many other areas. There are also programmes about healing on God Channel TV. Some towns now have Healing Rooms, based on the John G Lake Healing Rooms in Spokane, where people can go and be prayed for. Details of these will be available from the International Association of Healing Rooms, possibly online.

If a person's disability is as a result of some kind of accident, especially one that could be described as 'traumatic', it should be noted that there is a recognised 'spirit of trauma' which, if present, needs to be dealt with before healing power can be effective. This spirit seems to enter at the point of impact, etc, and has only recently been recognised as a destructive force. When it has been cast out, the person will generally go on to make a full recovery.

After receiving prayer, we need to confess our healing and avoid any negative speaking, even though nothing seems to have happened. Not all healing is immediate and the power must be given time to be effective and maintained with positive speech. Proverbs 18:21 says, **'Life and death are in the power of the tongue'** and we have already discussed the power of speech in some detail. By the same token, it is best to avoid people who may speak negatively about us. 'Negaspeak' at the wrong time can effectively put us into doubt mode and destroy our progress.

It is a good idea to speak out Bible passages

that confirm our healing and keep the power 'switched on' by calling those things that are not yet as though they were. We have already established that this is God's way. We should continually thank God for the manifestation of the healing that is there for us, as described in Yonggi Cho's *Fourth Dimension*, and our faith will draw it into being.

Having made sure once again that we have no unrepented unforgiveness, we should check our habits for anything which might be hindering our healing. We need to maintain a healthy diet, get sufficient sleep and try to avoid overworking by having a rest day. Smoking damages our health and so does anxiety and worry. We must try to 'be anxious for nothing' (Phillippians 4:6) and leave things to God, who is faithful and sure to carry out His Word. We should make sure we have nothing to do with idolatry or witchcraft (fortune telling is not as harmless as it looks). We should make sure we honour our parents and be faithful to tithe. Walking in love towards others is very important as it is a New Commandment, so we are told by

Jesus in John 13:34. We must be certain of what God's Word says about our healing and spend time in it getting to know Him. If we get our priorities right and spend time getting into right relationship with God, He will do the rest. If we are taking medication prescribed by a doctor, we should not stop taking it unless we have a very clear word from God. We should wait for our healing to manifest and let the doctor stop our medication. It will be a witness to him as well. We should gently begin to do things we have been unable to do, increasing gradually, unless our healing is miraculous and we are immediately totally free of all symptoms.

When we are asked how we are, it is tricky to know how to reply, and we should be very cautious. 'Healed and whole in the name of Jesus' is quite a useful reply that leaves us free not to discuss symptoms. We should remember the devil is still prowling about looking for someone to devour, and nothing would give him more satisfaction than to get us back to square one. If we say we are healed, and healing is not yet manifested, it may cause unbelievers to scoff and lead us into doubt, so we must be very careful what we say and to whom. 'Better than I was, but not as good as I'm going to be' is a good cop out. Praising God and thanking Him for our healing is not telling lies, as some would have it, because scripturally we are all totally healed.

Whatever else we do, we should never, never give up on our healing. God never gives up on us and the least we can do is return the favour. He says in His Word, 'Choose life.' Is healing really a matter of choice? If God says it is, then it must be, whatever people may like to believe. What we see and what we feel, together with the experiences of others, none of these can change the Word of God. All we have to do is agree with Him, remembering that He sent His own Son to die an agonising death on the cross because we matter to Him. God's love to each of us is unconditional. His blessings are not, and we must seek to know what He requires of us.

To receive His very best for us, we need to get 'all the stones out of the way'. God bless you.

39203605R00085

Printed in Poland
by Amazon Fulfillment
Poland Sp. z o.o., Wrocław